Xamarin

Building Your First Mobile App with C# .NET and Xamarin

4nd Edition

Introduction

The Xamarin platform is currently one of the most important mobile application development platforms available, which seems to remain on the forefront of time, especially after the acquisition of Microsoft company, which also has the same name (Xamarin). You may be motivated to enter the mobile app development world (as when you first got acquainted with Xamarin) and ready to write code directly, but to be patient a little, and to understand the beginnings, and the principle of Xamarin working better within this article, which is the first in a series that will guide you to How to develop applications using Xamarin platform and create practical applications through them.

Xamarin (read Zamarin) was founded in 2011 by the same engineers who designed the Mono project. The Mono Brothers project like Mono for android and Mono Touch are platforms to run applications written in C # on the operating systems: Linux, Android and iOS respectively. With Xamarin, you can create native Native Apps for Android, iOS, Mac and Windows in a programming language that isn't officially supported. In this series, we'll focus on building Android apps.

Whose series?

If you have a good familiarity with C Sharp and BCL within the DotNet framework, as well as a basic knowledge of how to use the Visual Studio 2015 development environment, and are passionate about learning how to program mobile apps using Xamarin, this series is definitely for you. Here at the Hassoub Academy we have a C-Sharp educational series that can be used.

Need for Xamarin

The need for Xamarin has arisen because of the nature of mobile applications and their work on different operating systems from competing companies. There are currently three different operating systems dominating the market: iOS for Apple, Android

for Google, and Windows Phone for Microsoft. These systems differ in many respects, which we will discuss below.
User experience

For the user experience there is a similarity in these systems in terms of providing the graphical user interfaces and interacting with the device through touch or multi-touch, but there are differences in the details. Each operating system has different ways of navigating application pages, presenting data, working with menus, and other details that require a developer to take a different approach for each operating system.
Development environments and different programming languages

For programming languages and development environments, this is another matter. Each operating system has its own requirements, which I quickly summarize as follows:

 - To create applications on iOS you need to master the Objective-C programming language or the Swift programming language. And own a MacBook (any version) with the Xcode development environment.
- To create applications on Android you will need Java with the Android Studio development environment running on many operating systems.
- To create applications running on Windows Phone or Windows 10 Mobile, you need the C # programming language with a computer running Windows, and the Visual Studio development environment.

Different programming interfaces

All previous operating systems rely on different APIs. However, there are some similarities for user-interface objects. For example, all previous systems provide a way for the user to choose a Boolean logical state that can be represented as True or False.In iOS, this object is classified as a view named UISwitch, in Android it is a widget called Switch, and in Windows it is called ToggleSwitch.

The solution provided by Xamarin

All of the above points can be bypassed by Xamarin because it provides a single programming language, C-Sharp, that can be used to write applications on any operating system. It also provides a single advanced development environment, Visual Studio 2015, for writing these applications (the Xamarin Studio development environment can also be used for Mac). In addition, it unified the various APIs into a single developer interface.

The C-Sharp language is defenseless. It is a strong, flexible, very rich and enduring language. It has truly become one of the most advanced and modern programming languages. We are not here to prefer a programming language over another, but in my personal experience, and to know many other programming languages, you can say that Sea Sharp occupies a prominent position among them. For a specific application, developers can write one common code for all previous operating systems without any modifications to them in terms of business logic within the application and the software operations that are not related to the type of mobile device or operating system it is running on. We call this code independent of platform independent. If the application is required to handle the hard hardware of the device it is working on (such as a camera or a GPS sensor), then you can write parts of the code that take into account the specificity of each operating system, we call such code as the code associated with the platform dependent operating system.
The main components of the platform Xamarin

Since its inception, Xamarin has focused on the technology of compilers. The company has released three core sets of .NET libraries: Xamarin.Mac, Xamarin.iOS and Xamarin.Andorid, which together make up the Xamarin platform. These libraries allow developers to write native apps for each of the supported operating systems.

Xamarin models

In 2014, Xamarin created what is known as Xamarin or Xamarin Forms. This platform allows developers to write user interface code so that it can be converted directly into applications running on Android, iOS and Windows. In fact, Xamarin Forms now supports generic Universal Windows Platform applications on devices running different Windows versions such as Windows Phone, Windows 10, Windows 10 Mobile, Windows 8.1, and Windows 8.1 Phone.

The solution architecture in Visual Studio will not change much, except that the separate projects for previous operating systems will be remarkably small due to the small amount of code in them. In this case, the PCL or SAP project will include the shared code, independent of the operating systems as agreed earlier, as well as the code responsible for displaying and handling the user interface. In other words, Xamarin Forms allows us to write a single code that works directly on different operating systems. See the following figure to understand how Xamarin Forms applications work.

Applications written for different operating systems in this case rely entirely on the PCL or SAP project to communicate with the APIs. Thus in many applications it is possible to write only one code that works on all devices! Except where it is necessary to write custom code for a specific operating system. In the future this may change, it may be possible to write only one code that works on all devices of any kind. In this series we will talk about Xamarin Forms mainly.

How Xamarin works
For iOS applications, Xamarin's C-Sharp translator translates the code into MSIL, and then Apple's Mac translator is used to generate native native code running on iOS as if it were an object-C application.

For Android applications, the compiler will also generate the MSIL language, which in this case will create a common CLR for Android. The resulting applications in this case will also be very similar to those created using the Java language and Android Studio development environment for Android.

Finally, for apps running on Windows Phone and Windows 10 Mobile, apps are clearly supported, and will work like native apps created with Visual Studio without Xamarin.

Conclusion

The Xamarin platform is promising, and has a long history and rich experiences before Xamarin emerged. Microsoft may have realized its importance, and the acquisition was completed. I recommend that you take the initiative to learn Xamarin, especially if you are a C Sharp programmer, or have preliminary information about it. The coming days may bring more support and surprises to the Xamarin platform, the first of which was to make it free for personal use or small software teams. Starting with the next lesson in this tutorial, we will install Visual Studio 2015 and start working with Xamarin.

Chapter One
Application architecture

The structure of the application created using Xamarin

Run Visual Studio 2015, and after the main window appears go to the File menu and then to New and choose from the submenu that will appear Project option. As we did in the previous lesson, choose from the left side of the window that appears Cross-Platform, then choose Blank App (Xamarin.Forms Portable) from the middle section of the window. Give this project the name SimpleTextApp and click the OK button.

We will build a simple application that shows how to use a single Label to show text in Xamarin-based applications. From the

Solution Explorer, which is usually on the right side of the Visual Studio development environment window, just keep the SimpleTextApp.Droid and SimpleTextApp (Portable) projects because we will only handle Android applications (as we agreed from the previous lesson). You get a shape similar to the following:

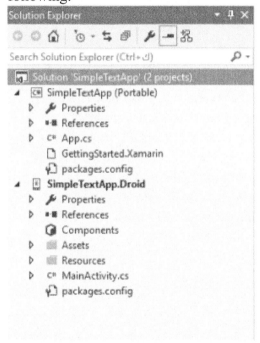

SimpleTextApp (Portable) contains most of the code, which is common behavior in PCL-style projects. The code within the project (with the Portable section plus its name) is common to all types of applications running on any operating system including Android. The basic .cs that will be present in any Xamarin application we talked about in the previous lesson and saw how it contains the App class that inherits from the Application class, and how the builder of that class is responsible for creating the application's home page. You will notice that there are several libraries that interest us These include: Xamarin.Forms.Core, Xamarin.Forms.Platform, Xamarin.Forms.Xaml These are the main libraries that are formed for Xamarin.Forms.

The SimpleTextApp.Droid project contains two folders: Assets and Resources. The Resources folder contains image files, layouts descriptions, and other files that are the resources for your app. Publish the Resources folder to see its structure. As for the Assets folder, the other public files that you want to include with your application are included. This project also contains the MainActivity.cs file, which contains a category with the same name as MainActivity, which is the main activity of the Android application. Open this file to find that this class contains the OnCreate function that is executed when you start the Android app. Note the following code statement within this function:

```
LoadApplication (new App ());
```

Obviously, it creates a new object from the App class within the SimpleTextApp (Portable) project and then passes it directly to the LoadApplication function to load the application and show it to the user. Creating a new object from the App class executes its structure and is responsible for creating the main page of the application as we have mentioned, however the idea will be well clarified after we start writing the code.

Write code
Right-click on SimpleTextApp (Portable) in the Solution Explorer to display a context menu, choose Add and then from the submenu Choose Class. The window for adding a new class will appear. Visual Studio will add a new file to the project named MainPage.cs that contains a class with the same name and content similar to the following:

```
using System;
using System.Collections.Generic;
using System.Linq;
using System.Text;
using System.Threading.Tasks;

namespace SimpleTextApp
{
class MainPage
{
```

```
}
}
```

We do not need most of the name ranges in the previous code in this program, we will currently need the domain name Xamarin.Forms. We will make the MainPage class inherit from the ContentPage class and add the builder to it. Modify the previous code to read as follows:

```
using Xamarin.Forms;

namespace SimpleTextApp
{
class MainPage: ContentPage
{
public MainPage ()
{
}
}
}
```

Note that I got rid of all unnecessary name ranges (however any unused name range will appear in the code in a faint color in the Visual Studio 2015 development environment). The MainPage class will play the role of a simple content page for the SimpleTextApp application. We will include in this category the code needed to create a single Label containing simple text. Then we will do some simple experiments on this label. This program is actually simple, and its mission is to make you more familiar with Xamarin.

We will start by creating a label from the Label class within the MainPage class builder. Labels are typically used to display text to the user. Look at the following simple code:

```
Label lblMain = new Label ();

lblMain.Text = "Welcome to moaml Academy!";
```

We create a label and create any object of a class. We set up a new code in the previous object of the class and Label Osndnah to the variable lblMain. Then Osndna text "! Welcome to Hsoub Academy" to the Text property of the variable lblMain. The Text property is used to set and read the text content of a list.

So that we can view the previous close-on the home page of the application, we assign variable lblMain to the Content property of the class ContentPage. Since the MainPage class inherits from the ContentPage, the Content property is automatically included within it. The attribution process will be as follows:

```
this.Content = lblMain;
```

Previous attribution process is possible because the class inherits from Label Class View, which represents a general view display interface concept. Since the Content property is also of type View, this attribution is possible. The contents of the MainPage.cs file will be similar to the following:

```
using Xamarin.Forms;

namespace SimpleTextApp
{
    class MainPage: ContentPage
    {
    public MainPage ()
```

```
        {
Label lblMain = new Label ();
lblMain.Text = "Welcome to moaml Academy!";

this.Content = lblMain;
        }
    }
}
```

That's it! Now we have to do a small step last, which is to make our application creates a new object of our brand as part of the MainPage file App.cs. Navigate to this file (located within the project (SimpleTextApp (Portable and make sure to be the builder of Class App on the following figure:

```
public App ()
{
// The root page of your application
MainPage = new MainPage ();
}
```

Now press the F5 key to execute the application, to get a shape similar to the following:

Welcome to moaml Academy!

Note:
You can connect your Android mobile device to your computer to try running the application directly on it. In this case, you should have an API installed on your computer suitable for the Android version on the mobile device. However, you can install this interface if it does not exist through the Android SDK Manager as noted in the previous lesson. I also recommend connecting mobile before running the Visual Studio development environment, or restarting it if it is already running.

Better code format:

In fact, the code found in the MainPage.cs file is not perfect, though simple. You may not feel a problem now, but when your programs get bigger, you will get into real problems because the previous method of writing code makes it very large. I will use the direct attribution feature while creating objects. This feature is useful in eliminating most of the variables in the program, which is limited to playing the role of a temporary intermediary. We will rewrite the code in the MainPage.cs file in a more elegant and practical way:

```
using Xamarin.Forms;

namespace SimpleTextApp
{
class MainPage : ContentPage
{
public MainPage()
{
this.Content = new Label{
Text = "Welcome to Hsoub Academy!"
};
}
}
}
```

Note that I dropped the lblMain variable because we assigned the Label object directly to the Content property.

Additional advantages over the app:

You will notice from the previous application that the sticker appears in the upper left corner of the window. We'll make it appear in the center of the screen. Two adjective properties should be set for this purpose: HorizontalOptions (for horizontal alignment options) and VerticalOptions (for vertical alignment options). Both of these properties are of type LayoutOptions, a struct structure that exists within the domain name Xamarin.Forms. This structure contains several ready-made fields that are useful for horizontal and vertical positioning options for the adhesion, which are very important options as we will see later in this series. Let us now make the required modification to the label within the MainPage class builder. The contents of the MainPage.cs file will look like this:

```
using Xamarin.Forms;

namespace SimpleTextApp
{
class MainPage: ContentPage
{
public MainPage ()
{
this.Content = new Label {
Text = "Welcome to Hsoub Academy!",
HorizontalOptions = LayoutOptions.Center,
VerticalOptions = LayoutOptions.Center
};
}
}
}
```

Notice that LayoutOptions.Center is assigned to HorizontalOptions and VerticalOptions for horizontal and vertical centering respectively. Run the program again You will notice that the sticker is in the center of the screen as shown in the following figure:

If you would like the text within the sticker to be a different color, say red, in this case, assign the Color.Red value to the TextColor property of the sticker object. Color is a structure within the Xamarin.Forms name range as well. See how to do it in the code:

```
this.Content = new Label {
```

```
Text = "Welcome to Hsoub Academy!",
HorizontalOptions = LayoutOptions.Center,
VerticalOptions = LayoutOptions.Center,
TextColor = Color.Red
};
```

Run the program again, to see the text become red.

Conclusion
In this lesson, we learned about the general structure of Xamarin within the Visual Studio 2015 development environment. We also built a very simple app called SimpleTextApp. The function of this app is to learn more about Xamarin. Starting with the next lesson, we will begin to build applications that are progressive in difficulty, with additional features that you can use as a mobile application programmer in your working life.

Chapter II
Working with texts

Text handling is a basic software task in all types of applications including mobile applications. Xamarin provides good techniques for dealing with texts, many of which will be covered in this lesson, as well as later lessons in this series. In this lesson, we'll address some of the situations a developer might encounter when working with text in apps they create.

Working with clips

We often need to display a bit of text on the screen. This text may come from a document, web service or other sources. The application should be able to handle texts of this size. As we did from the previous lesson, he created a new Blank App (Xamarin.Forms Portable) project called TextManipulationApp. Keep only the TextManipulationApp (Portable and TextManipulationApp.Droid) projects.

We will now add a new content page, but in a different and concise way than we did in the previous lesson. Right-click on the project (TextManipulationApp (Portable) and choose Add, then from the submenu that appears choose New Item. Choose from the left of the window that appears Cross-Platform node, and after updating the contents of the middle section of the window, choose the file type From the Name box at the bottom, click Add.

After Visual Studio adds this file, its contents will look like this:

```
using System;
using System.Collections.Generic;
using System.Linq;
using System.Reflection.Emit;
using System.Text;
```

```
using Xamarin.Forms;
namespace TextManipulationApp
{
public class ParagraphPage: ContentPage
{
public ParagraphPage ()
{
Content = new StackLayout
{
Children = {
new Label {Text = "Hello ContentPage"}
}
};
}
}
}
```

There are unnecessary name domains here but are currently ok.
Note that the ParagraphPage class inherits from the ContentPage
class by default, and that the ParagraphPage class builder is ready
and has a simple example ready. Delete the contents of this
builder, let's start working on our app. We will create a Label that
contains a text clip written in Arabic. Type the following code into
the ParagraphPage class builder:

```
Content = new Label
{
VerticalOptions = LayoutOptions.Center,
    Text = "Xamarin is currently one of the most important mobile
app development platforms available," +
"Which seems to stay on the front for not too long," +
"Especially after Microsoft acquired the company that also has the
same name." +
"Through this series we will learn to write practical applications
by using this promising technology."
};
```

Go to the App.cs file within the TextManipulationApp (Portal) project and make sure that the app class builder looks like this:

```
public App ()
{
// The root page of your application
MainPage = new ParagraphPage ();
}
```

Run the program using F5

Note that all text is aligned vertically in the middle of the screen. The reason for this is to assign the LayoutOptions.Center value to the VerticalOptions property of the Label. Also note that the text in the previous figure is aligned to the left, not to the right as expected for Arabic texts. This is because the HorizontalTextAlignment property of the Label class, which is responsible for the horizontal alignment of text within a label, will have the default value of TextAlignment.Start when running the program. TextAlignment is a number of enum with three values: Start, Center, and End. Since the screen of the mobile device is divided into three main areas horizontally: Start for the left area, Center for the central (central) area and End for the right area of the screen so the text will be aligned to the left instead of to the right. If we want to align the text to the right, all you have to do is assign the TextAlignment.End value to the HorizontalTextAlignment property, which we will do shortly. Another thing to note from the previous figure is that the text is so close to the edges of the screen that it almost sticks to it. The solution to this topic is simple: adding padding to the edges of the screen, a small area that can be programmatically assigned to the screen, from which we can control the margin space on its four sides. Now look at the ParagraphPage class builder with the required modifications:

```
public ParagraphPage ()
```

```
{
Content = new Label
{
VerticalOptions = LayoutOptions.Center,
Text = "Xamarin is currently one of the most important mobile
app development platforms available," +
"Which seems to stay on the front for not too long," +
"Especially after Microsoft acquired the company that also has the
same name." +
"Through this series we will learn to write practical applications
through the use of this promising technology.",

HorizontalTextAlignment = TextAlignment.End
};

Padding = new Thickness (5, 5, 5, 5);
}
```

We first added the HorizontalTextAlignment property to the Label
and assigned the TextAlignment.End value to align the text within
the label to the right (note that the regular comma separates
properties). We also added the Padding property (from the
ParagraphPage class) and assigned it a new object of the
Thickness class. Thickness is subject to overloading as it has more
than one shape. I used the last figure that accepts four arguments
representing padding amounts from left, top, right and bottom,
respectively. You may wonder about one analogy used here, but I
will postpone the discussion around it to a later lesson. When you
execute the program you will get the desired format

Now notice how the text is aligned to the right (within the Label), and also notice how the text moved away from the edges of the screen after setting the Padding property of the ParagraphPage content page.

Note: Please distinguish the HorizontalOptions and HorizontalTextAlignment properties of the Label. The first represents the horizontal positioning options of the image within the screen. The second represents the horizontal alignment of the text within the text. In the same way, the VerticalOptions and VerticalTextAlignment properties of the Label must be distinguished but vertically rather than horizontal.

Formatting text within a sticker
The text in the Label can be formatted as we would like by using another attribute of the label: FormattedText.

The FormattedText property is of the FormattedString class, which in turn has a property named Spans of type <IList <Span. It is a collection (list) of objects of type Span. Any Span object that coordinates a specific portion of the total text, is controlled by six properties of the Span class: the text portion to be formatted, the font name FontFamily, the font size FontSize, the font attributes FontAttributes, the ForegroundColor text color, and the BackgroundColor color.

If you feel some confusion from the previous speech is fine! We'll explain these in a simple example that adds some effects to the text that appears on the screen

```
using System;
using System.Collections.Generic;
using System.Linq;
using System.Reflection.Emit;
using System.Text;

using Xamarin.Forms;
```

```csharp
namespace TextManipulationApp
{
public class FormattedParagraphPage: ContentPage
{
public FormattedParagraphPage ()
{
FormattedString formattedString = new FormattedString ();

formattedString.Spans.Add (new Span
{
Text = "Don't count",
});

formattedString.Spans.Add (new Span
{
Text = "Glory",
BackgroundColor = Color.Yellow,
ForegroundColor = Color.Blue,
});

formattedString.Spans.Add (new Span
{
Text = "Pass you eat",
});

formattedString.Spans.Add (new Span
{
        Text = "You will not attain glory until you lick
patience.",
        ForegroundColor = Color.Aqua,
        FontSize = Device.GetNamedSize (NamedSize.Large,
typeof (Label))
});

Content = new Label
{
VerticalOptions = LayoutOptions.Center,
FormattedText = formattedString,
```

HorizontalTextAlignment = TextAlignment.End,
FontSize = Device.GetNamedSize (NamedSize.Medium, typeof
(Label))
};

Padding = new Thickness (5, 5, 5, 5);
}
}
}

We started in the builder (line 15) by creating an object of the FormattedString class and assigning it to the formattedString variable. We then started adding formatted text to the Spans menu using the following simple method (lines 17 to 20):

formattedString.Spans.Add (new Span
{
Text = "Don't count"
});

We used the Add function from the Spans menu to add an object of type Span where we created this object and assigned the Text property to it directly upon creation. The text in the previous code does not carry any special formatting. In fact, we have repeated this method for each part of the full text. But we sometimes adopted some different text formats. See, for example, the code in lines 22 through 27:

formattedString.Spans.Add (new Span
{
Text = "Glory",
BackgroundColor = Color.Yellow,
ForegroundColor = Color.Blue,
});

This time we coordinated the text "Glory" so that we assigned yellow as the background color for BackgroundColor, and blue for the text color ForegroundColor. See also the text portion we added in lines 34 to 39:

```
formattedString.Spans.Add (new Span
{
Text = "You will not attain glory until you lick patience.",
ForegroundColor = Color.Aqua,
FontSize = Device.GetNamedSize (NamedSize.Large, typeof
(Label))
});
```

This time the font color Aqua and font size Large. Notice how we assigned the font size value to the FontSize property. The following expression was used for this purpose:

Device.GetNamedSize (NamedSize.Large, typeof (Label))

Device represents the current device on which our application works, and contains many useful static functions. From these functions we used the GetNamedSize function, which returns the font size required by the arguments passed to it. The first argument is NamedSize.Large, so we want a large font size (NamedSize is numbered), and the second argument is the type of element to apply this font to. In this case we want to apply this line to the Label so we passed typeof (Label) as the second argument where the Type of Label returns. This is the preferred method of setting the appropriate measurements for anything that comes to your mind, because the devices we are working on will be differently measured screens , So we want to let the GetNamedSize function do the right calculations to return the appropriate font size relative to the screen size the program is currently working on, and to the size to be obtained (in our example we wanted to get a large font size NamedSize.Large and other measurements are definitely there).

The rest of the program is very easy, in line 44 we assign the formattedString variable to the FormattedText property of the property. This ensures that the text is formatted on the screen, noting that we did not use the Text attribute in this case.

One last thing to pay attention to. Note that in line 46 we assign a new font size to the FontSize property of the label. This font will be medium in size (note the first argument, NamedSize.Medium). The idea here is that this font will be applied to each piece of text (contained within a Span object) if the FontSize property of that part is not set. For example, this size will not apply to the part of the text specified in lines 34 to 39. This part has set its own font size (NamedSize.Large) as we saw earlier.

Note: To try this program, you will need to modify the App Builder within the App.cs file. Make sure the builder looks like this to use our new class FormattedParagraphPage:

```
public App ()
{
// The root page of your application
MainPage = new FormattedParagraphPage ();
}
```

Conclusion
In this lesson, we introduced the principles of text processing in Xamarin and built for the first time two simple applications that show some information to the user. We learned how to align text and make some formatting operations such as changing the text color and background color of any word or phrase. This lesson did not address how to handle a situation where the text is large and needs a way to pass it to display its entire contents. We will address this issue in a later lesson

Chapter III
StackLayout in Xamarin

In the previous lessons, we dealt with only one element that appears on the screen. This element was a Label that we assigned to the Content property of a content page. In real programs as is known, we will definitely need many elements that will appear on the screen to meet the requirements of the program. The problem here is that the Content property of a content page only accepts one element that inherits from the View class.

Xamarin has found a simple solution to this problem using layouts. A chart can accommodate any number of items that each inherits from the View class. In fact, the chart itself inherits from the Layout <View> class and this class inherits indirectly from the View class. Any content schema can be directly assigned.
Xamarin supports four types of charts:

AbsoluteLayout
- **GridLayout**
- **RelativeLayout**
- **StackLayout stack layout.**
 We will look at three schemes in this series: Mutlaq, Reticular and Stacked. In this chapter we will begin with the StackLayout stack diagram.

StackLayout stack layout:

Any number of items can be added to this chart. The reason for this name is because it arranges stacked elements. The StackLayout class has two additional properties from the rest of the charts: Orientation, which expresses the direction (horizontal or vertical) and Spacing, and represents the spacing between the elements added to the chart and has a default value of 6.0. Let us now take a simple example of how to deal with this useful scheme.

ColorsApp application to display some colors
Create a new app as we learned from previous lessons so that it is of type Blank App (Xamarin.Forms Portable) and named ColorsApp. After you create the application in Visual Studio, keep only the ColorsApp (Portable) and ColorsApp.Droid projects.
Add to the Project ColorsApp (Portable) a content page named ColorsListPage (right click on the project and choose Add and choose New Item. After the window appears, choose Cross-Platform from the left, and from the center of the screen choose Forms ContentPage). After creating this page we will notice that it already has a stacked layout ready. See the contents of this page:

```
using System;
using System.Collections.Generic;
using System.Linq;
using System.Reflection.Emit;
using System.Text;

using Xamarin.Forms;

namespace ColorsApp
{
    public class ColorsListPage: ContentPage
    {
        public ColorsListPage ()
        {
            Content = new StackLayout
            {
                Children = {
                    new Label {Text = "Hello ContentPage"}
                },
            };
        }
    }
}
```

Notice how we assign a new object from the StackLayout class to the Content property within the ColorsListPage builder. Also note how the StackLayout schema has a property called Children that expresses the child elements (each inheriting from the View class) that we would like to add to the stack. Replace the contents of the ColorsListPage.cs file with the following code:

```
using System;
using System.Collections.Generic;
using System.Linq;
using System.Reflection.Emit;
using System.Text;

using Xamarin.Forms;
```

```csharp
namespace ColorsApp
{
public class ColorInfo
{
public Color Color {get; set; }
public string Name {get; set; }
}

public class ColorsListPage: ContentPage
{
public ColorsListPage ()
{
ColorInfo [] colors = new ColorInfo []
{
new ColorInfo {Color = Color.Aqua, Name = "Aqua"},
new ColorInfo {Color = Color.Blue, Name = "Blue"},
new ColorInfo {Color = Color.Gray, Name = "Gray"},
new ColorInfo {Color = Color.Black, Name = "Black"},
new ColorInfo {Color = Color.Silver, Name = "Silver"},
new ColorInfo {Color = Color.Red, Name = "Red"},
new ColorInfo {Color = Color.Maroon, Name = "Maroon"},
new ColorInfo {Color = Color.Yellow, Name = "Yellow"},
new ColorInfo {Color = Color.Olive, Name = "Olive"},
new ColorInfo {Color = Color.Lime, Name = "Lime"},
new ColorInfo {Color = Color.Green, Name = "Green"},
new ColorInfo {Color = Color.Navy, Name = "Navy"},
        new ColorInfo {Color = Color.Teal, Name = "Teal"},
new ColorInfo {Color = Color.Pink, Name = "Pink"},
new ColorInfo {Color = Color.Fuchsia, Name = "Fuchsia"},
new ColorInfo {Color = Color.Purple, Name = "Purple"}
};

StackLayout stackLayout = new StackLayout ();

for (int i = 0; i <colors.Length; i ++)
{
stackLayout.Children.Add (new Label
```

```
{
Text = colors [i] .Name,
            TextColor = colors [i] .Color,
FontSize = Device.GetNamedSize (NamedSize.Large, typeof
(Label))
});
}

Padding = new Thickness (5, 5, 5, 5);

Content = stackLayout;
}
}
}
```

We've added a new simple class named ColorInfo to this file (lines 11 through 15). Although having two classes in the same file is usually bad software, I opted for simplification. The function of this class is to keep simple information about any color value and its name. In line 21, we created an array of the ColorInfo class and assigned it to the colors variable. This matrix will obviously have 16 colors. We then create a new object of the StackLayout class and assign it to the stackLayout variable (line 41), then enter a for loop (line 43) that passes over the elements of the colors array. To the stackLayout stack by adding the child property of it. Next, determine the amount of padding for the page (line 53) and eventually assign the stackLayout variable to the page's Content property (line 55). To try this app, first go to the App.cs file and make sure the App class builder looks like this:

```
public App ()
{
    // The root page of your application
    MainPage = new ColorsListPage ();
}
```

Run the program using F5 to get a look similar to the following:

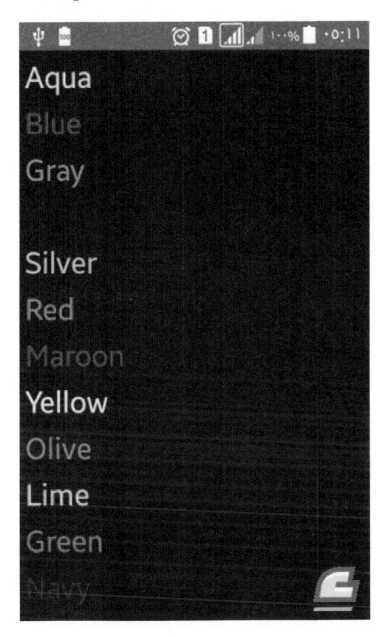

Here are two important things. The first is that some colors do not appear well on the black background (the default background for Xamarin apps in Android) because the color contrast is not good, but the word Black will not appear because the color is similar to the black background color. As for the second thing, we have basically 16 colors, but only 12 of them appeared. The number of colors you see may vary depending on the screen you are using.It may all appear for example, but in any case you will definitely encounter apps in the future where not all items will appear at once on the screen. In fact, we need a scrolling mechanism like any other Android app. We will now address both of the above.

Enhanced ColorsApp implementation

We will first address the color variation that can be solved by adding a new function to the ColorsListPage class named GetSuitableBackground. The function of this function is to calculate the amount of luminance according to the numerical constants that are recognized as ideal. If the illumination of the color to be shown is greater than 0.5, the background will be black; if less than or equal to 0.5, the background will be white. This gives an appropriate contrast to the colors displayed on the screen. See the code for this function:

```
private Color GetSuitableBackground (Color color)
{
    double luminance = 0.30 * color.R +
            0.59 * color.G +
            0.11 * color.B;

    return luminance> 0.5? Color.Black: Color.White;
}
```

The color.R, color.G, and color.B properties express the red, green, and blue components, respectively, of the color passed to this function to which the appropriate background color is to be found. The 0.30, 0.59 and 0.11 constants are ideal for finding color lighting and you can change them if you like.

As for scrolling the screen, it's simple to use ScrollView where we create a new object, assign the stackLayout variable to the Content property of that object, and then assign that new object to the Content property of the ColorsListPage instead of assigning stackLayout directly to it as we did. In the previous program. Look at the following code:

```
Content = new ScrollView
{
    Content = stackLayout
};
```

Now look at the full code after making the previous modifications:

```
using System;
using System.Collections.Generic;
using System.Linq;
using System.Reflection.Emit;
using System.Text;

using Xamarin.Forms;

namespace ColorsApp
{
    public class ColorInfo
    {
        public Color Color {get; set; }
        public string Name {get; set; }
    }

    public class ColorsListPage: ContentPage
    {
        public ColorsListPage ()
        {
            ColorInfo [] colors = new ColorInfo []
            {
                new ColorInfo {Color = Color.Aqua, Name = "Aqua"},
                new ColorInfo {Color = Color.Blue, Name = "Blue"},
                new ColorInfo {Color = Color.Gray, Name = "Gray"},
```

```
            new ColorInfo {Color = Color.Black, Name = "Black"},
            new ColorInfo {Color = Color.Silver, Name = "Silver"},
            new ColorInfo {Color = Color.Red, Name = "Red"},
            new ColorInfo {Color = Color.Maroon, Name =
"Maroon"},
            new ColorInfo {Color = Color.Yellow, Name =
"Yellow"},
            new ColorInfo {Color = Color.Olive, Name = "Olive"},
            new ColorInfo {Color = Color.Lime, Name = "Lime"},
            new ColorInfo {Color = Color.Green, Name =
"Green"},
            new ColorInfo {Color = Color.Navy, Name = "Navy"},
            new ColorInfo {Color = Color.Teal, Name = "Teal"},
            new ColorInfo {Color = Color.Pink, Name = "Pink"},
            new ColorInfo {Color = Color.Fuchsia, Name =
"Fuchsia"},
            new ColorInfo {Color = Color.Purple, Name =
"Purple"}
        };

        StackLayout stackLayout = new StackLayout ();

        for (int i = 0; i <colors.Length; i ++)
        {
            stackLayout.Children.Add (new Label
            {
                Text = colors [i] .Name,
                TextColor = colors [i] .Color,
                BackgroundColor = GetSuitableBackground (colors
[i] .Color),
                FontSize = Device.GetNamedSize (NamedSize.Large,
typeof (Label))
            });
        }

        Padding = new Thickness (5, 5, 5, 5);

        Content = new ScrollView
```

```
        {
            Content = stackLayout
        };
    }

    private Color GetSuitableBackground (Color color)
    {
        double luminance = 0.30 * color.R +
                    0.59 * color.G +
                    0.11 * color.B;

        return luminance> 0.5? Color.Black: Color.White;
    }
  }
}
```

Consider the previous code, and make sure you understand it well. Then run the program using F5 to get a look similar to the following. I used the new scrolling feature to show the rest of the elements that were not shown before with us:

Silver

Red

Maroon

Yellow

Olive

Lime

Green

Navy

Teal

Pink

Fuchsia

Purple

You will notice that each color shown in this list has a background color suitable for it to be optimized.

Note
You can use the Spacing feature of the stack chart to increase or decrease the amount of spacing between labels on the screen. Spacing has the default value of 6.0, as mentioned above. Try to set the value to 0, for example, and see what happens. You can set this property for the previous program by adding the following line:

stackLayout.Spacing = 0;

Immediately after the next line:

StackLayout stackLayout = new StackLayout ();

Conclusion
In this lesson, we learned about the principles of dealing with the StackLayout stack diagram, which is widely used in Xamarin applications to arrange the visual elements on the screen stacked. We also learned how to stack the stack layout so we can display items that don't appear on the screen. We will continue our work with the stack plan in the next lesson, where we will talk about more important advantages that this scheme has.

Chapter IV
Screen measurements

In this lesson in the Xamarin mobile application programming series, we will talk about an important topic that often causes some confusion for mobile app developers, which is dealing with measurements and sizes on the screen. We will first start with a quick historical overview, moving on to understanding the units of measurements used in Xamarin.Forms.

Historical overview
Any projector consists of a rectangular array of Pixels. Any object displayed on the screen will have a pixel area. From the outset, programmers treated pixels as a standard measurement to draw different objects and shapes on the screen. Although the programmer should not usually rely on fixed measurements of the visual elements in the applications he writes, it is often necessary

to do so as required by the application. With different screen sizes and different pixel density per screen due to technical advances in this field, it is becoming a major challenge for programmers to have the same shape on different displays.

Desktop monitors have a wide range of pixel measurements, from the old 640x480 (640 pixels wide, 480 pixels tall) to these days reaching a few thousand per dimension. The monitors also have a physical measurement, usually in inches, the diagonal distance of the screen rectangle. By measuring and physically measuring any pixel of a screen, we can calculate the resolution of pixels per inch (PPI), often called DPI (Dots Per Inch).

For example, for an old 800x600 pixel screen, we can simply conclude that according to Pythagoras's theorem in the existing triangle, this screen is 1000 pixels in diameter.

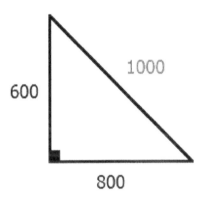

600

1000

800

In contrast, for the same 13-inch screen, we can now find pixel measurements such as 2560x1600, which gives the DPI of this screen an approximate 230. This means that any object on the new screen, say, 100 square pixels, for example, will occupy a third of the virtual space occupied by the body itself but on the old screen, which will lead to a significant difference in the forms of applications on different monitors.

Practical solutions are beginning to emerge with the development of desktop operating systems, which were later adapted to mobile devices. Companies like Microsoft and Apple have devised measurement systems based on non-device-independent units rather than pixels. It is incumbent upon the operating system to convert these measurements designed with the new measurement system to suitable pixel measurements. Thus, programmers can write applications based on an independent measurement system, so that their applications appear almost uniformly on different types of screens.

Google in Android followed the same behavior to ensure that formats with specified sizes would appear uniformly on all Android screens of various genres.

The solution provided by Xamarin.Forms:

Xamarin.Forms provided a good solution to this issue with the following simple hypothesis: every 160 units (device independent) correspond to one inch. This is equivalent to 64 units of measurement per centimeter. The above hypothesis is valid for any application running on Android, iOS or Windows Phone.

Any visible object that appears on the screen inherits from the VisualElement class. This category has two useful features: Width and Height. These properties express the width of the Width and the height of any visible element on the screen in units independent of the device as we agreed. The initial value of each is -1 at the beginning, and gives us valid values only when the layout that appears on the screen is processed and each element takes its place.

The VisualElement class also defines an event named SizeChanged that occurs when the value of one of the Width or Height properties changes. These values may change for a variety of reasons, such as rotating the screen.

It is possible to install a handler for the SizeChanged event for any visual element that appears on the page, including the page itself. In the following section, we will cover a simple program that shows the measurement of the screen on which it works, but in units independent of the device.

Software to get screen measurement
Create a new Blank App (Xamarin.Forms Portable) application
and name it GetSize. As agreed, delete all projects except GetSize
(Portable) and GetSize.Droid. Add a new ContentPage to the
GetSize (Portable) project and name it GetSizePage and make sure
the GetSizePage class looks like this:

```
public class GetSizePage: ContentPage
{
private Label label;

    public GetSizePage ()
{
this.label = new Label
{
FontSize = Device.GetNamedSize (NamedSize.Large, typeof
(Label)),
HorizontalOptions = LayoutOptions.Center,
VerticalOptions = LayoutOptions.Center,
};

Content = this.label;

SizeChanged + = GetSizePage_SizeChanged;
}

private void GetSizePage_SizeChanged (object sender, EventArgs
e)
{
label.Text = String.Format ("{0} \ u00D7 {1}", this.Width,
this.Height);
}
}
```

Note at the beginning that we have declared the label field of type
Label in line 3, where we will assign a reference to a new tag that
we will create later in the GetSizePage class builder in line 7. The

reason for creating this field is the need to access the label within the event handler as we will see shortly. . We assigned the HorizontalOptions and VerticalOptions options on lines 10 and 11 respectively for this new label to appear in the center of the page. Note that we do not use a stacked layout in this program, but we assign the adjective directly to the page's Content property in line 14. The new thing for us in this series is to assign an event handler to the SizeChanged event of the page in line 16. The event handler I called GetPageSize_SizeChanged is declared in Lines 19 through 22.

If you look at line 21 you will find that we are generating formatted text to display within the list (we assign it to its Text property). Note the \ u00D7 code used to generate the multiplication sign x as we will see shortly. Note that we read the page's Width and Height properties and include them in the generated formatting text. Go to the App Builder and make sure it is as follows:

```
public App ()
{
    // The root page of your application
    MainPage = new GetSizePage ();
}
```

Run the program using F5 to get a look similar to the following:

I would like to emphasize that the measurement you see in the previous figure is in units independent of the device and not in pixels. It does not include the top status bar, nor does it include the space for the buttons to appear below (if the device supports it). If you try to rotate the screen 90 degrees. You will get different measurement

-The logo is not part of the result

Note
You have run the previous program on your Samsung Galaxy Core Prime.

Conclusion
This lesson is essential for understanding how to deal with measurements in Xamarin.Forms applications where we talked about measurements in their old and new concepts. Ways of dealing with device-independent units and their essential role in standardizing the measurements of visual elements with fixed dimensions on different types of screens. In the next lesson, we will find useful practical examples of using standalone modules to write two simple applications. The first application deals with drawing a simple shape with a specific area on the screen, while the second application deals with a simple digital clock that matches the text displayed according to the size of the screen on which the application works.

Chapter V
Tap events on the screen

In the preceding chapters in this series, we deal with visual elements whose primary function is to display data appropriately to the user. In fact there is another type of visual element, including those elements that the user can interact with to perform a particular command or task. In this fun chapter we will look at the Button element, a visual element that allows a user to click (or rather touch) a particular command.

Counter application
It is a simple application, intended to understand how to handle buttons in Xamarin.Forms. The interface of this application

consists of two buttons in addition to a sticker. The idea of the application is simple. When a user clicks one of the buttons, the number displayed on the label increases by one, and when he clicks on the other button, that number decreases by one too. Create a new Blank App (Xamarin.Forms Portable) application as usual and name it CounterApp, and keep only the CounterApp.Droid and CounterApp (Portable) projects within it. Add a new ContentPage content page named CounterPage. Make sure that the content of the CounterPage.cs file is as follows:

```
1 using System;
2 using Xamarin.Forms;
3
4 namespace CounterApp
5 {
6    public class CounterPage : ContentPage
7    {
8        private int counter = 0;
9        private Label lblDisplay;
10
11       public CounterPage()
12       {
13           Button btnIncrement = new Button
14           {
15               Text = "+",
16               HorizontalOptions = LayoutOptions.CenterAndExpand,
17               FontSize = Device.GetNamedSize(NamedSize.Large, typeof(Label))
18           };
19           btnIncrement.Clicked += btnIncrement_Clicked;
20
21           Button btnDecrement = new Button
22           {
23               Text = "-",
24               HorizontalOptions = LayoutOptions.CenterAndExpand,
```

```
25          FontSize = Device.GetNamedSize(NamedSize.Large,
typeof(Label))
26        };
27        btnDecrement.Clicked += BtnDecrement_Clicked;
28
29        lblDisplay = new Label
30        {
31            Text = "0",
32            TextColor = Color.Accent,
33            HorizontalOptions =
LayoutOptions.CenterAndExpand,
34            FontSize = Device.GetNamedSize(NamedSize.Large,
typeof(Label))
35        };
36
37        Content = new StackLayout
38        {
39          Children = {
40              new StackLayout
41              {
42                  Orientation = StackOrientation.Horizontal,
43                  Padding = new Thickness(0,64,0,64),
44                  Children =
45                  {
46                      btnIncrement,
47                      btnDecrement
48                  }
49              },
50              lblDisplay
51          }
52        };
53    }
54
55    private void BtnDecrement_Clicked(object sender,
EventArgs e)
56    {
57        counter--;
58        lblDisplay.Text = counter.ToString();
```

```
59      }
60
61      private void btnIncrement_Clicked(object sender,
EventArgs e)
62      {
63          counter++;
64          lblDisplay.Text = counter.ToString();
65      }
66  }
67}
```

Note
Remember that we are adding a new content page by right-
clicking on the CounterApp (Portable) project and then selecting
Add and then New Item. From the window that appears, choose
Cross-Platform from the left section, and from the right section we
choose Forms ContentPage

We have encountered many of the techniques used in this
application in the previous lessons. With some new things. For
example, for the first time we have developed a stacked layout
among others, which is very common in the design of facades.
In line 8, we declare the counter field, which is the counter that
will keep the current value of the number displayed in the list. We
will need each of the two previous fields within different
dependents of the CounterPage class so we put them in the form of
two fields for this image.
In the CounterPage builder, we declare the btnIncrement of the
Button type and assign it a new Button-type object where we
assign the property values directly upon creation. Note that on line
19 we have assigned the Clicked event handler for this button. The
name of this handler is btnIncrement_Clicked, which is stated
below in lines 61 through 65. The same is true for the
btnDecrement button (lines 21 through 27) and its event handler
btnDecrement_Clicked (lines 55 to 59). By one and display the
result within the adhesion.

If we go to the Content property of the CounterPage class (line 37), a new stack chart is assigned and it has a default vertical orientation as we explained in a previous lesson. We will assign it only to Children (line 39). This feature states that there are two sons to this scheme, the first son is another stacked planner (lines 40 to 49), and the second is the lblDisplay, which will display the current issue:

```
Children = {
    new StackLayout
    {
        Orientation = StackOrientation.Horizontal,
        Padding = new Thickness(0,64,0,64),
        Children =
        {
            btnIncrement,
            btnDecrement
        }
    },
    lblDisplay
}
```

As for the Stacked Son Scheme as shown in the last code, note that we set the Orientation property to be horizontal StackOrientation.Horizontal, we have a suitable padding padding from the top and bottom of its content, and finally we assigned the Child property to it so that it has two sons here with the increase buttons btnIncrement and decrease btnDecement Clear.
The stacked son (inner) scheme would then have two buttons located horizontally in the middle, and the father's (stacked) stacked plan would contain a stacked son scheme, and a sticker vertically positioned.
Go to the App.cs file and make sure the App class builder looks like this:

```
public App ()
```

```
{
    // The root page of your application
    MainPage = new CounterPage ();
}
```

When you execute the program using F5, you will get a look similar to the following, I made several clicks on each of the buttons:

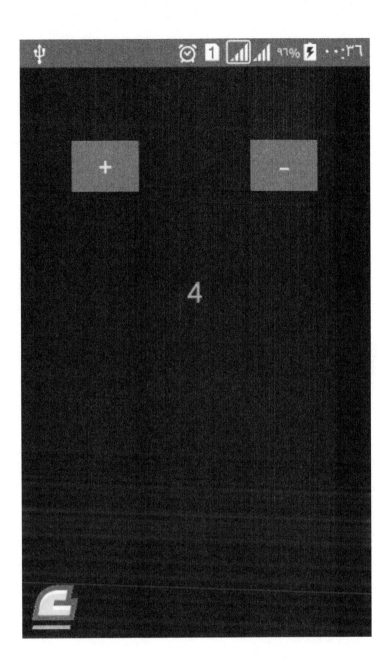

Conclusion

In this lesson, we dealt with the principles of dealing with buttons in Xamarin.Forms through two basic applications that interact with the user. In addition to talking about how to display custom messages to the user using the function DisplayAlert. There are many advantages of buttons in Xamarin.Forms. We will review later in this series for more additional features of the buttons as well as other visual elements that the user can interact with.

Chapter VI
Image processing in Xamarin

As we know, images are essential elements of any application, they add aesthetic touch and give an explanatory impression of the basic functions of the application. We will continue our work in this series by explaining how to use images in Xamarin.Froms. Xamarin deals with bitmaps that may differ slightly for Android, iOS, and Windows, but if you rely on formats like JPEG, PNG and BMP, you won't have any problems.

Xamarin.Forms handles images in two main styles. The first method relies on platform-independent images, and the second method relies on platform-specific images or, more precisely, the operating system. You will address the first method in our lesson through two simple applications that illustrate this. The second method will be postponed to another lesson.

Images within Xamarin applications can be viewed by a visual element represented by the Image class. As with other visual elements that inherit from the VisualElement class, this element has many properties in common with any other visual element, such as the Label. In addition to other features that distinguish it, such as the Source property, which reflects the source of the image that will be displayed within it. This feature will be our focus in this lesson. Device independent images can be obtained in two different styles. In each method, you need to assign an object of the ImageSource class to the Image property of the Image object.

The first method is to get images directly from the Internet, by calling the FromUri static function from the ImageSource class and passing the Uri address of the image file online.

The second method is to invoke the FromResource static function from the ImageSource class and pass the resource name to it. The following two simple applications will explain how to do this.

Get a picture from the Internet:

Create a new app called WebImageApp of type Blank App (Xamarin.Forms Portable) and keep only the WebImageApp (Portable) and WebImageApp.Droid projects as we have already agreed. Add a new ContentPage as we did in this lesson. Name it WebImagePage and make sure that the contents of the WebImagePage.cs file are as follows:

```
using System;
using Xamarin.Forms;

namespace WebImageApp
{
  public class WebImagePage: ContentPage
  {
    public WebImagePage ()
    {
      Image webImage = new Image
      {
        VerticalOptions = LayoutOptions.FillAndExpand,
        HorizontalOptions = LayoutOptions.FillAndExpand,
        Source = ImageSource.FromUri (new Uri
("https://developer.xamarin.com/demo/IMG_2138.JPG?width=80
0")),
        Aspect = Aspect.AspectFit,
        BackgroundColor = Color.Accent
      };

      Content = new StackLayout
      {
        Children = {
          webImage
        }
      };
    }
  }
}
```

Then navigate to the App.cs file and make sure that it looks like this:

```
public App ()
{
    // The root page of your application
    MainPage = new WebImagePage ();
}
```

The application code is simple, it creates a new image object, assigns it to the webImage variable, and then makes that image object a child of the stack layout clearly.

What we are interested in now is the properties of the image object. The Source property is the source from which we get the image. In this application we will get the image from the Internet so we will use the static function ImageSource.FromUri that returns an object from the ImageSource row. Note that we've passed a new Uri object to this function:

ImageSource.FromUri (new Uri ("https://developer.xamarin.com/demo/IMG_2138.JPG?width =800"))

The address used here is:

"https://developer.xamarin.com/demo/IMG_2138.JPG?width =800"

Aspect specifies how the image is displayed within the Image element. They accept values from the Aspect of the same name. This number has three elements: AspectFit, AspectFill and Fill. In this application we used the AspectFit value which is the default value. Here's what the three previous values mean:

* AspectFit: means that the image will appear within the element so that it is consistent with the space allocated to it, while respecting the aspect ratio of the image appearance.

* AspectFill: In this case the image will appear within the element so that the aspect ratio of the image will be respected, but it will not take care of the space allocated to this element. Therefore, the image may appear truncated if it is larger than the element.

* Fill: This value means that the image will appear to occupy the entire area allocated to the object without regard to the aspect ratio of the image. So just the image appears stretched horizontally or vertically. You have assigned Color.Accent to the BackgroundColor property of the image element in order to see the actual space occupied by that element. Run the previous program using F5 to get a look similar to the following, noting that I'm testing on a device with a 4.5-inch screen, so the results you get on your device may vary if you have a larger screen. If so, I recommend deleting the "? Width = 800" section of the image's Uri title from the Source property:

Notice how the image appeared so that the space remained empty from the top and bottom. This is because it respected the aspect ratio of the original image. If you modify the Aspect property to carry the value Aspect.AspectFill, you will get a look similar to the following:

Notice here how the image appeared slightly truncated. Now try the last case, assigning the value Aspect.Fill to the Aspect property to get a shape similar to the following:

As expected, the image appeared to be stretched vertically because it would fill the entire space available for the image element without regard to the proportion of the appearance of the original image as noted.

Get a picture from a local resource:

Working with images in this method is no different from the way we handle images we get from the web. Except that we use the FromResource static function of the ImageSource class. In this section, we'll discuss a practical application to browse through a set of images that I have created specifically for this purpose. You will be browsed by two buttons: "Next" and "Previous", in addition to a sticker showing a simple information about the current image number displayed on the image element. These images will be locally located within the app. Now let's start by creating a new app called ResourceImageApp of type Blank App (Xamarin.Forms Portable). Keep only the ResourceImageApp (Portable) and ResourceImageApp.Droid projects. Add a new content page named ContentImagePage and make sure the contents of the ResourceImagePage.cs file are as follows:

```
1 using System;
2 using Xamarin.Forms;
3
4 namespace ResourceImageApp
5 {
6    public class ResourceImagePage : ContentPage
7    {
8       private Button btnPrev;
9       private Button btnNext;
10       private Image resourceImage;
11       private Label lblInfo;
12       private int currentIndex = 1;
13
14       public ResourceImagePage()
15       {
16          lblInfo = new Label
17          {
18             VerticalOptions = LayoutOptions.Start,
19             HorizontalOptions = LayoutOptions.FillAndExpand,
20             HorizontalTextAlignment = TextAlignment.Center,
```

```
21          TextColor = Color.Accent,
22          FontSize =
Device.GetNamedSize(NamedSize.Medium, typeof(Label))
23       };
24
25       resourceImage = new Image
26       {
27          VerticalOptions = LayoutOptions.FillAndExpand,
28          HorizontalOptions = LayoutOptions.FillAndExpand,
29          Aspect = Aspect.AspectFit
30       };
31
32       btnPrev = new Button
33       {
34          Text = "first",
35          HorizontalOptions = LayoutOptions.FillAndExpand,
36          IsEnabled = false
37       };
38       btnPrev.Clicked += BtnPrev_Clicked;
39
40       btnNext = new Button
41       {
42          Text = "next",
43          HorizontalOptions = LayoutOptions.FillAndExpand
44       };
45       btnNext.Clicked += BtnNext_Clicked;
46
47       StackLayout buttonsLayout = new StackLayout
48       {
49          Orientation = StackOrientation.Horizontal,
50          VerticalOptions = LayoutOptions.End,
51          HorizontalOptions = LayoutOptions.FillAndExpand,
52          Children =
53          {
54             btnNext,
55             btnPrev
56          }
57       };
```

```
58
59        Content = new StackLayout
60        {
61          Children = {
62            lblInfo,
63            resourceImage,
64            buttonsLayout
65          }
66        };
67
68        Padding = new Thickness(5, 5, 5, 5);
69
70        UpdateScreen();
71      }
72
73      private void BtnPrev_Clicked(object sender, EventArgs e)
74      {
75        currentIndex--;
76        if (currentIndex == 1)
77        {
78          btnPrev.IsEnabled = false;
79        }
80
81        btnNext.IsEnabled = true;
82
83        UpdateScreen();
84      }
85
86      private void BtnNext_Clicked(object sender, EventArgs e)
87      {
88        currentIndex++;
89        if (currentIndex == 5)
90        {
91          btnNext.IsEnabled = false;
92        }
93
94        btnPrev.IsEnabled = true;
95
```

```
96         UpdateScreen();
97      }
98
99      private void UpdateScreen()
100     {
101         lblInfo.Text = string.Format("5 {0} ", currentIndex);
102         string path =
string.Format("ResourceImageApp.Images.res0{0}.jpg",
currentIndex);
103         resourceImage.Source =
ImageSource.FromResource(path);
104     }
105   }
106}
```

Then navigate to the App.cs file and make sure that it looks like this:

```
public App ()
{
   // The root page of your application
   MainPage = new ResourceImagePage ();
}
```

Right-click on the ResourceImageApp (Portable) joint project and choose Add and from the side menu that appears choose New Folder. This will create a new volume within this project, called Images. Then right-click on our new Images folder and select Add. Choose image files: res01.jpg, res02.jpg, res03.jpg, res04.jpg, res05.jpg (click here to download Images.zip). The images in this order contain the words "Welcome to Hassoub Academy". Right-click again on each file name you just added to the project and from the menu select Properties. The file properties will appear, set the Build Action property to Embedded Resource as shown in the following file format:

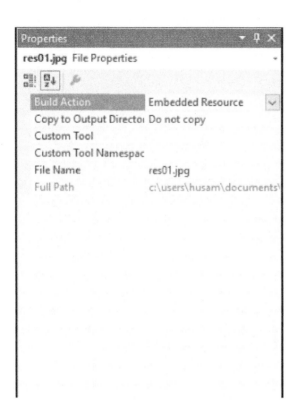

Once you click the Back button, the Next button will be back up. Let's discuss the operating code for this application. Note in lines 8 through 11 that I have stated special fields that represent most of the visual elements that we will deal with in this application, a picture element and a close element and two buttons for the next and previous. In line 12, you declare a special variable currentIndex that represents the current file number that we would like to display in the image file and has a preliminary value of 1. The ResourceImagePage class structure configures all the visual elements used as we know. In lines 16 through 23, we set the properties of the lblInfo label where we assign the LayoutOptions.Start value to the VerticalOptions property so that the first (top) of the screen appears. We also assigned the TextAlignment.Center value for the HorizontalTextAlignment property so that the text would appear horizontal. As for the resourceImage image element, we set its properties in lines 25 through 30 where we set the Aspect property value to Aspect.AspectFit to fill the image space available with respect to the proportion of the appearance of the image. Next comes the adjustment of the btnPrev (previous) and btnNext (next) buttons from lines 32 to 45. Later, we will add these buttons to their stacked layout, buttonsLayout, which is why we want to make these buttons adjacent horizontally and fill the horizontal space available to them. Note the LayoutOptions.FillAndExpand value for the HorizontalOptions property for both). We announce the stackLayout layout on lines 47 through 57. We will add to this chart the buttons btnPrev and btnNext and set the Orientation property to be horizontal StackOrientation.Horizontal to show the previous two buttons horizontally and not vertically. We will add this stack layout shortly to the basic stack layout of the page.

We set the content property of the page in lines 59 to 66 so that we create a new stack chart that contains the elements: sticker, image, and stack layout of buttons, respectively. This is why previous items appear in this order. Look at the following diagram showing the approximate position of the previous items on the page:

The brown rectangle at the bottom represents the stack layout of buttonsLayout

The btnPrev (lines 73 to 84) and btnNext (lines 86 to 97) buttons have simple programmatic logic that ensures proper navigation between the five images within the application resource. Finally, the UpdateScreen function (lines 99 to 104) updates the data that appears on the close and image elements at each click of the Next and Previous buttons. The FromResource function of the ImageSource class requires a text argument that represents the file ID. The file ID consists of the name of the application (or more precisely the Assembly) followed by a period, the name of the folder containing the image file, followed by another point, and finally the name of the file with its extension. In our example, the file ID res01.jpg is as follows:

ResourceImageApp.Images.res01.jpg

The code of this app may look relatively large, but I assure you that you will write a few times in any commercial program that you can work on! This is due to the approach we have taken from the beginning of this series so far, relying on the code to create the entire user interface. Although it is possible to use good methods that contribute to the arrangement and organization of this code significantly, many developers prefer to use the other method in the development of applications using Xamarin.Forms, which is the use of XAML (code-like XML), which allows to separate the user interface from the code Software. We will, of course, deal with this in future lessons.

Conclusion

In this lesson we dealt with images in Xamarin.Forms. We discussed the issue from two different sides. The first aspect is to download the image from the Internet (and possibly from a local network), while the second aspect is to download the image from a local source. There is more to talk about in this topic, especially with regard to the acquisition of images through the sources of images associated with the device platform-specific or more precisely associated with the operating system running on the device, which is the Android system in our case. This is similar to the method used when working with image sources through Android Studio. We will cover this topic later in this book.

Chapter VII
Move between pages

Mobile apps typically consist of separate pages that the user navigates to take advantage of the capabilities the app offers. For Android apps, the Back button is essential in this navigation. In this tutorial from the Xamarin.Forms Android Application Programming Learning Series, we learn how to navigate between application pages. First we will talk about the concept of page navigation in a single application, and then we will talk about the types of content pages used in navigation through a simple practical example.

The concept of navigating between application pages
Navigating between application pages is very similar to the
principle that Stack works. The stack is known as a data structure
that supports the concept of LIFO (which finally comes out first).
When you move from page A to page B, page B is pushed to the
top of the stack, resulting in the user appearing. Similarly, when
you move from page B to page C, page C is pushed to the stack to
be shown to the user. When we want to return to the original page
A, popped page C should be removed from the stack, page B will
be at the top of the stack (i.e. it will appear to the user), and page
B will be removed from the stack and page A will be at the top of
the stack. See the following figure to illustrate this idea:

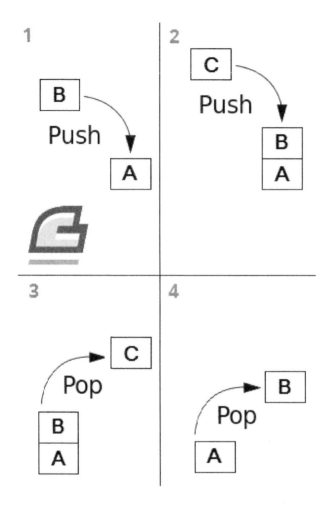

Modal and Modeless Pages:

Each application contains a main page (which will be in the category NavigationPage) is the main node from which all other pages, whatever their number and level, can be accessed. Xamarin also distinguishes two types of content pages that are used within this navigation structure: Modal Pages and Modeless Pages. The difference between these two types for Android apps is simple. That is, in Modal pages, the title of the page will not be displayed at the top as we will see in the example shortly. In a Modeless page, the title of the page will be at the top if it is specified using the Title property of the content page. To preview the difference between these types, let's create a simple, practical application that illustrates this. Start by creating a new Blank App (Xamarin.Forms Portable) project called ModelessAndModal, then just keep the ModelessAndModal (Portable) and ModelessAndModal.Droid projects as we did in this lesson. Next we will add three regular content pages (Forms ContentPage): MainPage, ModalPage and ModelessPage. Edit the contents of the MainPage file to be similar to the following:

```
1   using Xamarin.Forms;
2
3   namespace ModelessAndModal
4   {
5       public class MainPage : ContentPage
6       {
7           public MainPage()
8           {
9               Title = "Main Page";
10
11              Button gotoModelessButton = new Button
12              {
13                  Text = "Go to Modeless Page",
14                  HorizontalOptions = LayoutOptions.Center,
15                  VerticalOptions = LayoutOptions.CenterAndExpand
16              };
17
18              gotoModelessButton.Clicked += async (sender, args)
    =>
19              {
20                  await Navigation.PushAsync(new ModelessPage());
21              };
22
23              Button gotoModalButton = new Button
24              {
25                  Text = "Go to Modal Page",
26                  HorizontalOptions = LayoutOptions.Center,
27                  VerticalOptions = LayoutOptions.CenterAndExpand
28              };
29
```

```
30            gotoModalButton.Clicked += async (sender, args) =>
31            {
32                await Navigation.PushModalAsync(new
ModalPage());
33            };
34
35            Content = new StackLayout
36            {
37                Children = { gotoModelessButton, gotoModalButton
}
38            };
39        }
40    }
41 }
```

The MainPage will display only two buttons. The first button is
gotoModelessButton and its function is to create a modeless non-
rigid page and navigate to it. The second button is
gotoModalButton and its function is to create and navigate to a
static modal page. For the first button gotoModelessButton look at
lines 11 through 21:


```
Button gotoModelessButton = new Button
{
   Text = "Go to Modeless Page",
   HorizontalOptions = LayoutOptions.Center,
   VerticalOptions = LayoutOptions.CenterAndExpand
};

gotoModelessButton.Clicked + = async (sender, args) =>
{
   await Navigation.PushAsync (new ModelessPage ());
};
```
We first create a Button object and assign it to the
gotoModelessButton variable, and then assign a clicked event
handler, a simple lambda expression that represents a function that
needs a sender and e argument, preceded by the reserved word

async, as shown in the previous code. The reason async exists is because we'll use an asynchronous call within this event handler:

await Navigation.PushAsync (new ModelessPage ());

The PushAsync function called from the Navigation property of the current page pushes a new page within the stack to move between pages. In the previous line, a new page of type ModelessPage will be created and passed to the PushAsync child. I recommend you review this lesson to refresh your memory on the topic of asynchronous calls. The same will be done for the button to go to the static page with a nuance. This time, the call will be via PushModalAsync (line 32) to move to a static page (ModalPage). In each of the two previous cases, we could have the two click processors within independent dependencies and not as with Lambda. Also noteworthy for the MainPage class is the title property set (line 9). In fact, this feature has had no meaning in all the programs we have created in this series so far. Setting this feature or not will make no difference! What's new here is how to create the MainPage page itself, which we will create as usual within the App class. Go to the App.cs file and make sure that it looks like the following:

```
public App ()
{
    // The root page of your application
    MainPage = new NavigationPage (new MainPage ());
}
```

Notice with me the new command here. We don't create a content page and assign it to the MainPage property just as we used to. We create a content page (in our example it is from the MainPage class) and then pass this page as an intermediary to the NavigationPage class builder. That is, we are actually creating a content page that supports navigation. This will make the title of the home page set with the title property appear at the top of the page as we will see shortly. We can now try this app. Run the app to get a look like this:

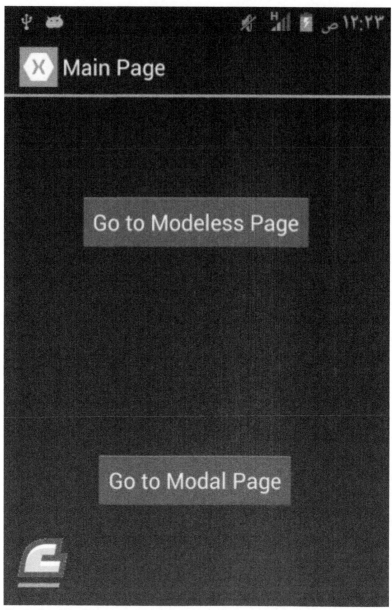

Stop the implementation of the program to begin with the final stage of preparing the content pages ModalPage and ModelessPage. Go to the ModalPage.cs file and make sure that its contents match the following:

using Xamarin.Forms;

```
namespace ModelessAndModal
{
    public class ModalPage: ContentPage
    {
        public ModalPage ()
        {
            Title = "Modal Page";
            Button goBackButton = new Button
            {
                Text = "Back to Main",
                HorizontalOptions = LayoutOptions.Center,
                VerticalOptions = LayoutOptions.Center
            };

            goBackButton.Clicked + = async (sender, args) =>
            {
                await Navigation.PopModalAsync ();
            };

            Content = goBackButton;
        }
    }
}
```

Then navigate to the ModelessPage.cs file and make sure its contents are as follows:

```
using Xamarin.Forms;

namespace ModelessAndModal
{
    public class ModelessPage: ContentPage
    {
        public ModelessPage ()
        {
            Title = "Modeless Page";
            Button goBackButton = new Button
            {
                Text = "Back to Main",
```

```
            HorizontalOptions = LayoutOptions.Center,
            VerticalOptions = LayoutOptions.Center
        };


        goBackButton.Clicked + = async (sender, args) =>
        {
            await Navigation.PopAsync ();
        };


        Content = goBackButton;
    }
  }
}
```

The contents of each of the previous two pages are identical. Each
has a button called goBackButton that is intended to return to the
previous page (which caused the current page to appear). There is
only one slight difference between the two click event handlers on
the previous two pages. For the modal page, the
navigation.PopModalAsync call was used to return to the previous
page. For the modeless page, Navigation.PopAsync was used to
return to the previous page. Another difference when executing
the program is that if you move from the home page to the
ModelessPage page, the page title will appear at the top with a
small arrow that allows us to return to the previous page. When
you go from the home page to the ModePage page, the title of the
page will never appear (although the Title property is set to it).
The only way to return to the previous page is by clicking the back
button on the page or by clicking the back button provided by the
operating system. . Experiment with the app and see the difference
between the two pages.

Conclusion
In this lesson we discussed how to navigate between pages in
Android apps, which is of course an important topic. We've
identified the difference between modal and modeless pages. We
also learned how to create the master page, which is the main

building block in the transition between pages, by creating the master page to be NavigationPage.

Chapter VIII
Engineering Transformations

Transforms are essential mathematical concepts in the world of graphic programming. There are three types of engineering conversions:

- **Withdrawal**
- **Rotation**
- **Emulating Scale**

Geometric conversions are based primarily on matrices. They are important mathematical structures that are the backbone of any geometric transformation. Fortunately, Xamarin simplifies it and makes it easy to use the previous three conversions. In this lesson from the series on learning Android application programming using Xamarin.Forms, we will talk about each of the three previous types and how to implement it in a simple practical example.

Withdrawal Translation:

Withdrawal is the transition without changing the size of the body, or making any rotation. Any element of the VisualElement class is rotated by the TranslationX and TranslationY properties. When assigning a positive value to the TranslationX property, this will move the object horizontally to the right (relative to its current location). When assigning a positive value to the TranslationY property, this will move the object vertically downward (relative to its current position). Let's start by testing this type of conversion. Start by creating a new Blank App (Xamarin.Forms Portable) project named TransformsApp, then just keep the TransformsApp (Portable) and TransformsApp.Droid projects as we did in this lesson. Next we will add a content page based on the XAML code, as we have already done in this lesson, we will call it TranslationPage. Make sure the contents of this page are as follows:

```
<ContentPage xmlns = "http://xamarin.com/schemas/2014/forms"
xmlns: x = "http://schemas.microsoft.com/winfx/2009/xaml" x:
Class = "TransformsApp.TranslationPage">
  <StackLayout Padding = "20, 10">
    <Frame x: Name = "frame" HorizontalOptions = "Center"
VerticalOptions = "CenterAndExpand" OutlineColor = "Accent">
      <Label Text = "TEXT" FontSize = "Large" />
    </Frame>
    <Slider x: Name = "xSlider" Minimum = "- 200" Maximum =
"200" Value = "{Binding Source = {x: Reference frame}, Path =
TranslationX}" />
    <Label Text = "{Binding Source = {x: Reference xSlider}, Path
= Value, StringFormat = 'TranslationX = {0: F0}'}"
HorizontalTextAlignment = "Center" />
```

```
<Slider x: Name = "ySlider"
        Minimum = "- 200" Maximum = "200" Value = "{Binding
Source = {x: Reference frame}, Path = TranslationY}" />
    <Label Text = "{Binding Source = {x: Reference ySlider}, Path
= Value, StringFormat = 'TranslationY = {0: F0}'}"
HorizontalTextAlignment = "Center" />
  </StackLayout>
</ContentPage>
```

The previous code uses the data-linking technology that we talked about in this lesson. It controls the location of a frame element with a sticker within it, via the Slider elements. The upper element controls the horizontal withdrawal, while the lower element controls the vertical withdrawal. This is done by linking the Value property of the Slider element xSlider to the TranslationX property of the frame element. Similarly, the Slider element, called ySlider, has a Value property associated with the TranslationY property of the frame element. Modify the App class builder in the App.cs file to read as follows:

```
public App ()
{
    // The root page of your application
    MainPage = new TranslationPage ();
}
```

Run the program to get output similar to the following:

Drag some experiments and note the cruise in this movement.

-Rotation

Any visible element in Xamarin can be rotated by selecting the center of rotation and angle of rotation. The angle of rotation is determined by degrees, and the positive values of the angle of rotation indicate the clockwise rotation. The rotation center of any element is determined by its AnchorX and AnchorY properties. The rotation angle can also be determined by Rotation. If no value is specified for the AnchorX and AnchorY properties, the center of rotation is the same as the center of the visible element by default. Let's see how this works by a simple example. Add to the current project a content page based on the XAML code, as we have already done in this lesson called RotationPage. Make sure the contents of this page are as follows:

```
<? xml version = "1.0" encoding = "utf-8"?>
<ContentPage xmlns = "http://xamarin.com/schemas/2014/forms"
        xmlns: x =
"http://schemas.microsoft.com/winfx/2009/xaml"
        x: Class = "TransformsApp.RotationPage">
  <StackLayout Padding = "20, 10">
    <Frame x: Name = "frame" HorizontalOptions = "Center"
VerticalOptions = "CenterAndExpand" OutlineColor = "Accent">
      <Label Text = "TEXT" FontSize = "Large" />
    </Frame>

    <Slider x: Name = "rotationSlider" Maximum = "360" Value =
"{Binding Source = {x: Reference frame}, Path = Rotation}" />

    <Label Text = "{Binding Source = {x: Reference
rotationSlider}, Path = Value, StringFormat = 'Rotation = {0:
F0}'}" HorizontalTextAlignment = "Center" />

    <StackLayout Orientation = "Horizontal" HorizontalOptions =
"Center">
      <Stepper x: Name = "anchorXStepper" Minimum = "- 1"
Maximum = "2" Increment = "0.25" Value = "{Binding Source =
{x: Reference frame}, Path = AnchorX}" />
      <Label Text = "{Binding Source = {x: Reference
anchorXStepper}, Path = Value, StringFormat = 'AnchorX = {0:
F2}'}" VerticalOptions = "Center" />
    </StackLayout>
```

```xml
<StackLayout Orientation = "Horizontal" HorizontalOptions = "Center">
    <Stepper x: Name = "anchorYStepper"
          Minimum = "- 1" Maximum = "2" Increment = "0.25"
Value = "{Binding Source = {x: Reference frame}, Path = AnchorY}" />
    <Label Text = "{Binding Source = {x: Reference anchorYStepper}, Path = Value, StringFormat = 'AnchorY = {0: F2}'}" VerticalOptions = "Center" />
    </StackLayout>

    </StackLayout>
</ContentPage>
```

The previous program relies on rotating a frame element containing a sticker. For this purpose, we will use a Slider named rotationSlider to control the angle of rotation (by associating with the Rotation property of the frame element). We will also use the Stepper elements anchorXStepper and anchorYStepper to control the coordinates of the spin center (by linking with the AnchorX and AnchorY properties of the frame element). To execute this program, go to the App class builder within the App.cs file and make sure to be as follows:

```csharp
public App ()
{
    // The root page of your application
    MainPage = new RotationPage ();
}
```

Run the program to get a look similar to the following:

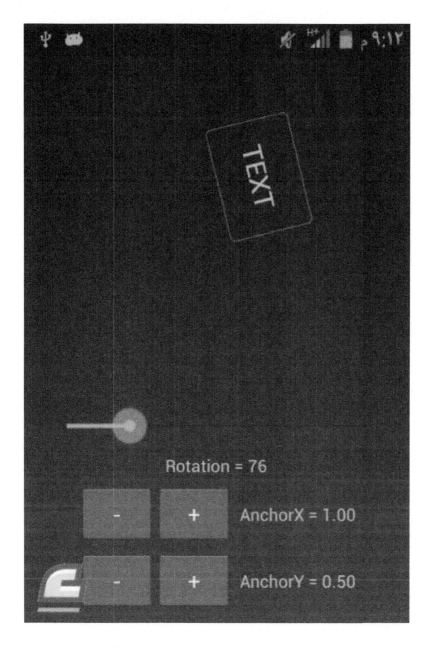

-     It's a great !
is not she ?

Do some experiments and enjoy the program!

Emulation Scale

Simulation is a geometric transformation that leads to change in sizes. The simulation can be used to control the sizes of visual elements via its Scale property. This property has a default value of 1. When using a value less than 1, we will reduce the size. When any value greater than 1 is used, we will enlarge the volume. For example, a value of 3 means we will magnify the volume 3 times, and so on. A value of 0 for the Scale property is allowed but will cause the element to disappear. Negative values of Scale can be used, but this will overturn the element while the previous concept remains the same. That is, a value of -1 will overturn the element but the volume remains the same. To simulate, add to the current project a content page based on the XAML code as we have already done in this lesson. Make sure the contents of this page are as follows:

```
<? xml version = "1.0" encoding = "utf-8"?>
<ContentPage xmlns = "http://xamarin.com/schemas/2014/forms"
        xmlns: x =
"http://schemas.microsoft.com/winfx/2009/xaml"
        x: Class = "TransformsApp.ScalePage">

  <StackLayout Padding = "20, 10">
    <Frame x: Name = "frame" HorizontalOptions = "Center"
VerticalOptions = "CenterAndExpand" OutlineColor = "Accent">
      <Label Text = "TEXT" FontSize = "Large" />
    </Frame>

    <Slider x: Name = "scaleSlider" Minimum = "- 10" Maximum
= "10" Value = "{Binding Source = {x: Reference frame}, Path =
Scale}" />

    <Label Text = "{Binding Source = {x: Reference scaleSlider},
Path = Value, StringFormat = 'Scale = {0: F1}'}"
HorizontalTextAlignment = "Center" />
  </StackLayout>

</ContentPage>
```

Go to the App class builder within the App.cs file and make sure it looks like this:

```
public App ()
{
    // The root page of your application
    MainPage = new ScalePage ();
}
```

Run the program to get a look similar to the following:

Conclusion:
In this lesson we talked about basic engineering transformations:
Translation, Rotation, Scale and how to deal with them through
Xamarin. In fact, the need for such conversions often lies in
gaming or graphical applications. We will apply some of these
conversions in the next lessons of this series.

Printed in Great Britain
by Amazon

76360215R00051